VALLEJO CITY UNIFIED SCHOOL DISTRICT
PENNYCOOK 45-15 YEAR ROUND SCHOOL
3620 FERNWOOD STREET
VALLEJO, CALIFORNIA 94590
543-8241

NUCLEAR POWER

Jacqueline Dineen

A description of how electricity is produced in power stations by an important source of power—the splitting of uranium atoms.

ENSLOW PUBLISHERS, INC.
Bloy St & Ramsey Ave.
Box 777
Hillside, N.J. 07205

Contents

Introduction   3

1. What is nuclear power?   5

2. How nuclear energy is produced   11

3. Radiation and radioactivity   19

4. Is nuclear power safe?   24

5. The future for nuclear power   29

Index   32

The picture above shows milk samples being collected from a farm near a nuclear power station for radiation monitoring.
[cover] The cover picture shows a laser being used to cut the wrapping from fast reactor fuel rods.
[title page] The picture on the title page shows the control room of a modern nuclear power station.
[1–25] All other pictures are identified by number in the text.

This series was developed for a worldwide market.

First American Edition, 1988
© Copyright 1986 Young Library Ltd

Printed in the United States of America

10 9 8 7 6 5 4 3 2 1

LIBRARY OF CONGRESS
Library of Congress Cataloging-in-Publication Data
Dineen, Jacqueline.
   Nuclear power / Jacqueline Dineen.
      p.   cm. -- (The world's harvest)
   Summary: Explains how nuclear energy is produced and discusses whether it is safe and where its future may lie.
   Includes index.
   ISBN 0-89490-220-2
   1. Nuclear energy--Juvenile literature.   [1. Nuclear energy.]
I. Title. II. Series: Dineen, Jacqueline. World's harvest.
TK9148.D56 1988
333.79'24--dc19
                                  88-1182
                                     CIP
                                      AC

Introduction

Most of our electricity is produced by burning coal or oil at power stations, but some is produced by another method called nuclear power. Nuclear power stations use a fuel called uranium, which is a mineral found in some types of rock. The uranium is not burned, like coal or oil. Nuclear power is produced by 'splitting atoms'. What does this mean? I explain this to you in the first chapter of this book.

In chapter 2, I tell you how uranium is mined in countries like Australia and Canada, in great opencast mines like the one in picture [1]. I explain how the uranium is treated in a

[1]

nuclear power station to produce great heat. This heat is used to make the steam which turns the generators. The generators produce electricity.

The main difficulty with nuclear power is that uranium is 'radioactive'. Radiation is a natural thing which is all around us, but too much can damage people's health. In chapter 3 I tell you what radiation is and how it is measured and monitored. I also tell you how it is used in beneficial ways, such as x-rays in hospitals.

Is nuclear power safe?

A big question which people ask about nuclear power is 'Is it safe?' In chapter 4 I tell you about the safety measures which governments and nuclear power stations have established. I describe how waste materials are stored and disposed of; how people who work in the nuclear industry are protected against the effects of radiation; and how the environment around nuclear power stations is checked to make sure that levels of radiation are not increasing.

Nuclear power is a useful alternative to coal and oil. Coal and oil are running out. We need to have some other fuel, otherwise one day we may have no way of making electricity. In chapter 5, I tell you how many countries in the world have nuclear power stations, and I describe other ways in which radioactive devices can be used. Research is going on all the time. Uranium is part of the world's harvest of natural minerals, and is too valuable to waste.

1 · *What is nuclear power?*

Most of the electricity we use in our homes is produced by burning oil or coal in power stations like the one in picture [2]. The heat from the burning fuels boils water to make steam. This steam rushes through pipes to turn the blades of a turbine. The turbine is connected to a generator.

A generator is a machine which produces electricity in huge amounts. The process is quite simple. On the generator shaft there is a magnet surrounded by copper bars. When the magnet spins, it generates an electrical current in the copper bars. The magnet has to spin very fast to do this, so the turbine which drives

A turbine is a motor consisting of a vaned wheel made to revolve very fast by the force of a jet of water (or steam, or expanding hot air), or by the strength of wind.

[2]

[3]

it must also spin very fast. That is why a lot of heat is needed to produce powerful jets of steam. Picture [3] shows the turbine and generator in a coal-fired power station.

Everybody is quite happy with this method of producing electricity. The problem is that the world's stocks of these fuels—coal and oil—will not last for ever. We must find new ways of producing electricity. One way is to use renewable energy sources, which I tell you about in another book in this series (*Energy from Sun, Wind, and Tide*). The other way is to use nuclear power.

There are already nuclear power stations in several countries. You can see one in picture [4]. The United States, Australia, Canada, Britain, France, Japan, and Russia all use nuclear power. So do several other countries. It is not very different from producing electricity by burning oil or coal. Great heat is produced, and this heat is used to make steam and drive a turbine. The difference is in the *way* the heat is produced.

The fuel used in nuclear power stations is called *uranium*. It is a mineral found in certain parts of the world, including Australia, Canada, the United States, and North Africa. The uranium is not burned, like coal and oil are. Instead, the 'atoms' which make up the uranium are split in a process called fission. When this happens, a very intense heat is produced.

Everything around us is made up of chemical substances called elements—and that includes you! They are the basic ingredients from which everything is made.

Each element is made up of very tiny particles called atoms. An atom is so small that you cannot see it, even with a microscope. Just think that the ink used to print a full stop (.) contains nearly 4 million atoms! It is difficult to imagine something as small as this.

In the early part of this century, scientists

7

found that atoms could be divided into three even tinier particles. At the centre of the atom are two groups of particles called neutrons and protons. This central part of the atom is called the nucleus. On the outside are moving particles called electrons. Look, for example, at picture [5] which shows an atom of a gas called helium.

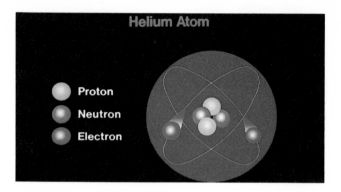

[5]

Helium is nothing like iron, yet both are made of atoms. So what makes atoms different from one another? The answer is that different types of atoms have different numbers of protons. For example, the number of protons in a carbon atom is not the same as the number of protons in an oxygen atom, or an iron atom, or a uranium atom. Every proton in an atom is balanced by an electron. If there are eight protons, there are also eight electrons.

Strong forces in the nucleus bind the neutrons and protons tightly together. The electrons spin round the outside, like planets going round the sun.

In 1939, German scientists discovered that

some uranium atoms can be split if an extra
neutron is added to the nucleus. This breaks
the 'nuclear' forces which hold the nucleus
together. Now you can see where the name
'nuclear power' comes from.

Splitting atoms is called the 'fission' process,
and it all sounds very complicated unless you
are a scientist yourself. The type of uranium
atoms which can be split are called uranium-
235 (U-235) atoms. Most of the uranium found
in the world is made up of U-238 atoms with
only about 1 per cent of the U-235 kind
sprinkled in it. U-238 atoms are slightly
different and they will not split.

Nuclear fission

    If an extra neutron is added to the nucleus
of a U-235 atom, the atom splits into two

[6]

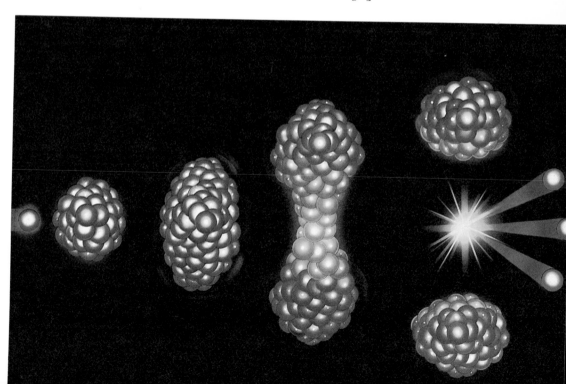

smaller atoms. It releases energy in the form of a very intense heat. At the same time, the split atom releases more neutrons. If one of these neutrons strikes another U-235 atom, that atom will split, and so the process continues. This is called a chain reaction. The fission process is shown in picture [6]. On the left is the extra neutron which joins the nucleus of the atom. On the right you can see three neutrons flying out as the atom splits.

In a nuclear power station, the fission process is controlled so that atoms keep splitting and constant heat is produced. I will tell you how this is done in the next chapter.

Nuclear fusion

There is one other way of producing heat from atoms. It is called nuclear fusion.

Uranium atoms are very heavy, in fact uranium is the heaviest of all elements. The atoms used in the fusion process are very light ones, such as hydrogen atoms. If these light atoms are heated to very high temperatures, the nuclei join (fuse) together and release large amounts of energy. The energy from the sun is produced by nuclear fusion. Researchers are trying to find ways of using nuclear fusion to produce electricity, but no power stations use this process at the moment.

It is very difficult to get the right conditions for the atoms to fuse because such enormous heat is needed to heat the gas. Think how hot the sun is. That is the sort of heat you need. Scientists are anxious to solve the problems because success with this method would end our worries about electricity supply in the future.

2 · *How nuclear energy is produced*

Uranium is a mineral found in rock such as granite. Thousands of tonnes of uranium ore have already been mined. Many parts of the world have not yet been surveyed for uranium because we have enough to keep us going at the moment. Like coal, uranium can not be replaced once it has been used up. However, when you think that 1 tonne of uranium can produce as much electricity as 25,000 tonnes of coal, you can see that we will never have to use it at such an alarming rate.

The uranium ore which comes out of the mine consists of a lot of rock and a small amount of uranium. At plants like this Australian one in picture [7], the uranium is

[7]

[8]

separated from the rock to produce a material called uranium oxide. Countries which have nuclear power stations import crude uranium oxide (yellowcake) from Australia, the United States, Canada, and North Africa. It is taken to a processing plant like the one in picture [8] to be turned into nuclear fuel.

I have already explained that only U-235 atoms will split and that uranium consists mostly of U-238 atoms. Some nuclear power stations use the uranium as it is, with less than 1 per cent of U-235 atoms. Others need a higher proportion than this. At the processing plant, some of the uranium is 'enriched' to give a higher proportion of U-235 atoms. Even so, only about 3 per cent of the atoms will split. It sounds as though a lot of uranium is wasted, but U-238 atoms can be turned into a new material called plutonium. Plutonium atoms split, just like U-235 atoms. I tell you more about this later.

The machine in which the atoms are split is called a nuclear reactor. There are two main types, thermal reactors and fast reactors.

Thermal reactors

Remember what I said in chapter 1 about how atoms are split. The neutrons are part of the nucleus of an atom. It is neutrons which make new atoms split. An extra neutron is added to the nucleus of a U-235 atom to start the process off. The atom splits, releasing heat and more neutrons. These neutrons hit more atoms and make them split in a 'chain reaction'.

Neutrons travel very fast when they are released from the nucleus of an atom. If they were left to themselves, they would shoot past most of the U-235 atoms without splitting them. In a thermal reactor, the neutrons are controlled so that they hit as many new atoms as possible. A 'moderator' is used to slow down the flying neutrons. Graphite (a type of carbon) is one of the moderators used. The uranium is made into rods and put into metal cans. You can see the rods being assembled in picture [9]. These fuel rods are placed in huge blocks of graphite in the reactor. The neutrons fly off the uranium rods and collide with the graphite atoms. This slows them down and diverts them back so that they collide with more U-235 atoms.

[9]

Boron is a solid, non-metallic element. Cadmium is a metal which is a bit like tin. When the boron or cadmium rods are lowered, they absorb spare neutrons and reduce the heat output. When more heat is needed, the rods are raised.

Neutrons which have been slowed down like this are called thermal neutrons. That is why reactors with moderators are called thermal reactors.

As the atoms split, more and more neutrons are released and things become hotter and hotter in the reactor. The heat also has to be controlled. Not all the neutrons that are flying around are needed to keep the chain going. The spare ones are 'mopped up' by rods of boron or cadmium.

When heat has built up in the reactor, a *coolant* is circulated through the system. In 'gas-cooled' reactors, carbon dioxide gas is blown through and becomes very hot. The gas takes the heat from the reactor to huge boilers full of water. The water boils and gives off steam which is used to turn the turbines.

Pressurised water reactors work in the same way, except that water is used as the moderator and as the coolant. The water is kept under pressure so that it does not boil and turn into steam. The water coolant carries the heat to a separate boiler to produce steam.

The earliest thermal reactors were called Magnox reactors. You can see the inside of a Magnox power station in picture [10]. They use natural uranium fuel (less than 1% U-235 atoms) and are cooled by carbon dioxide gas. They do not reach very high temperatures, so the advanced gas-cooled reactor (AGR) was introduced as a more efficient method. This reactor uses pellets of enriched uranium oxide with a higher proportion of U-235 atoms. The pressurised water reactor (PWR) has been developed in the United States and other

0]

countries and is cheaper to build than the AGR. Nearly half the world's nuclear power reactors are water-cooled.

Fast reactors

Each time an atom splits, two or three neutrons are released. Only one is needed to keep the chain reaction going. The neutrons which are not needed escape. Some are mopped up by the boron or cadmium rods I told you about earlier. Others are absorbed into the U-238 uranium and convert it into a dense metal called plutonium. Plutonium does not exist in nature, but it is made of atoms which will split and give out intense heat, just like U-235 atoms.

Thermal reactors cannot use plutonium efficiently, but another type of reactor—the fast reactor—can use plutonium. A fast reactor produces about 60 times as much energy as a thermal reactor.

The fuel used in fast reactors is a mixture of plutonium and uranium, packed into stainless steel cans like the ones in picture [11]. It is richer than uranium alone and so the chain reaction can be kept up without slowing down the neutrons. That is why it is called a 'fast' reactor. No moderator is needed, and liquid sodium (an element found in salt) is used to transfer the heat from the reactor to the boiler. This is more efficient than gas or water would be in a fast reactor.

A blanket of U-238 atoms is packed around the fuel rods. As spare neutrons fly off the fuel, they are caught in the U-238 blanket. The neutrons are absorbed into the U-238 and turn

[11]

it into more plutonium which can be used later. Over several years, a fast 'breeder' reactor can create as much plutonium as it uses.

The uranium in the reactor does not burn and disappear like coal. The rods still look the same as they did in the beginning, but the fuel becomes less efficient as the U-235 atoms are used up. After a few years they have to be replaced.

The spent fuel cannot just be thrown away. There are two reasons for this. One is that it would be wasteful because it can be recycled and used again.

When the spent fuel is taken out of the reactor it is stored in special ponds at the power stations, as you see in picture [12]. As

Recycling spent fuel

[12]

[13]

the fuel cools, the radioactivity lessens. Each 2 tonnes of fuel is packed into a 48-tonne container so that nothing will come in contact with the atmosphere. The fuel is then taken to a reprocessing plant and allowed to cool for a while longer. As you see in picture [13], everything has to be heavily shielded and operated by remote control so that people will not come into contact with the fuel.

The uranium consists of at least 96 per cent of 'unburnt' fuel which can be processed and used again. About 3 per cent is actual waste which is no more use. This is stored very carefully so that it can be disposed of safely. Picture [14] shows the process of recycling.

The other reason that the spent uranium cannot be thrown away is that it is dangerous because it is radioactive. I tell you about radioactivity in the next chapter.

[14]

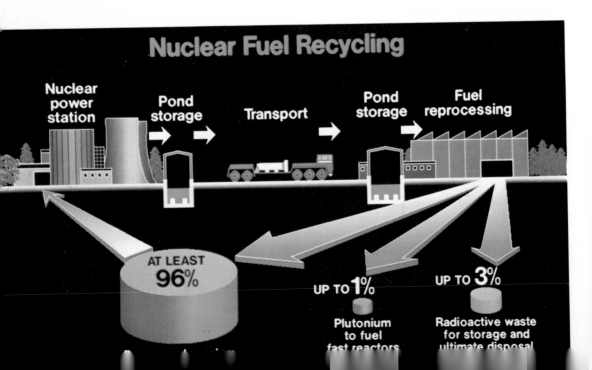

Nuclear Fuel Recycling

Nuclear power station → Pond storage → Transport → Pond storage → Fuel reprocessing

AT LEAST 96%

UP TO 1%
Plutonium to fuel fast reactors

UP TO 3%
Radioactive waste for storage and ultimate disposal

3 · Radiation and radioactivity

The word 'radiate' means 'to spread out rays', and 'radioactive' simply refers to something capable of sending out rays or minute particles at very high speed. Light, heat and radio waves are all forms of radiation. There are many types of radiation. In the world of nuclear energy, the type we are concerned with is 'ionising' radiation. Ionising radiation transfers electrically charged particles called ions to the objects it strikes. Too much ionising radiation can affect people's health, and even cause death. The materials used to produce nuclear power give off ionising radiation, and this is why some people are worried about it.

What exactly is a radioactive element? Remember that every element is made up of atoms which have a nucleus of protons and neutrons. Some of these atoms are 'stable' and others are 'unstable'. A 'stable' atom must have the right number of neutrons to balance the protons. Most of the things around us are made up of stable atoms, which never change. Some atoms do not have the right balance of protons and neutrons, and so they are unstable. It is these unstable atoms which are radioactive. They can disintegrate and send out tiny particles and rays called Alpha, Beta, and Gamma rays. You can see them illustrated in picture [15], and I will tell you in a moment what Alpha, Beta, and Gamma rays are.

How radioactivity can be dangerous

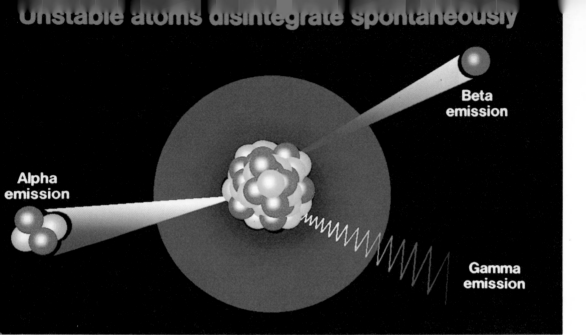

Beta emission

Alpha emission

Gamma emission

[15] Radioactive elements have always existed, so people have lived in a radioactive environment since the world began. Most natural radiation, such as that from sun, soil, and rocks, is absorbed into the earth's atmosphere. Even so, some is still taken into our bodies. This cannot be helped, but levels of radiation are always being checked. If people are exposed to too much of it, the cells and tissues of their bodies are damaged.

Radiation is not all bad, however. Scientists have learned to make artificial radioactive elements and these are a valuable part of the world today. Have you ever had an x-ray in a hospital? The equipment uses very powerful rays to see into your body. Radiation therapy is used for treating some illnesses by killing diseased cells. Television screens are coated with material which gives off light when struck by rays from radioactive material inside the set.

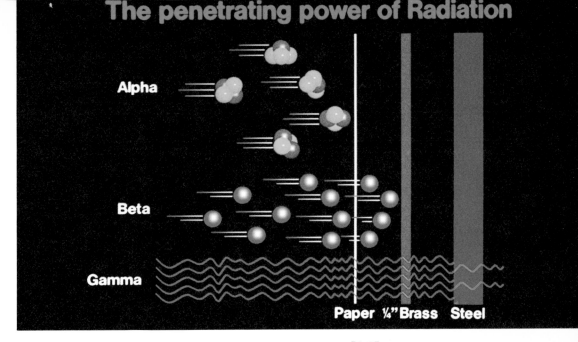

Alpha

Beta

Gamma

Paper ¼"Brass Steel

[16]

This sounds very alarming until you realise that there are different levels of radiation. We have survived the low-level natural radiation around us for thousands of years, and scientists do not think that it does us any harm.

The production of nuclear power causes a more intense type of radiation, known as high-level radiation. When atoms are split in a nuclear power station, they throw out radiations as fast-flying particles and rays. The three types of radiation sent out from the nucleus of radioactive atoms can be seen in picture [16].

Alpha radiations are streams of protons and neutrons. They travel a few centimetres in the air and cannot penetrate the skin. Their flight can be stopped by a sheet of paper, by clothing, or by your own body. However,

Alpha particles are dangerous if they are swallowed or breathed into the body.

Beta radiations are streams of electrons. They can travel a few metres through the air and can penetrate about 1 centimetre into the skin. A thin sheet of metal or glass can stop beta radiation.

Gamma rays are similar to x-rays and rays of light. They can go right through the body. Shields of thick concrete or lead can stop gamma radiation.

At nuclear power stations, there is also neutron radiation inside the reactors. Neutrons are very penetrating, like gamma rays, but they can be stopped by water or by thick concrete.

Of course, you cannot see any of these tiny particles flying through the air, but scientists can measure their radioactivity. Picture [17] shows a 'whole body' monitor. A person lies under the machine on the right, and the radioactivity in his body is measured by the instruments on the left.

The amount of radiation you receive depends on where you live. Some types of soil are richer in radioactive elements than others, for example. In Britain the average dose can be broken down into these percentages:

· Cosmic rays from outer space: 13
· Terrestrial rays from rocks and soil: 16
· Radioactive elements in our own bodies, and from eating, drinking and breathing: 16
· Radon gas inside buildings: 33
· Medical uses, mainly x-rays: 20.7
· Fall-out from nuclear weapons tests: 0.4

Radon is a gas given off as the radioactive element radium disintegrates.

[17]

· Miscellaneous (air travel, luminous watches, television sets etc.); 0.4
· Occupational (for people who work with radioactive material): 0.4
· Waste discharges from the nuclear industry: 0.4

You can see that most of the radiation we receive comes from our natural surroundings. The nuclear power industry plays a very small part. Even so, great care is taken to make sure that mistakes do not happen, and safety regulations are very strict.

4 · Is nuclear power safe?

Many people immediately think of 'the bomb' when the word 'nuclear' is mentioned and they are worried and suspicious about nuclear power. However, a nuclear reactor cannot blow up like a bomb. The worries about nuclear power are quite different from the worries about nuclear weapons.

What some people do not like about nuclear power stations is that the fuels—uranium and plutonium—are so radioactive.

Plutonium is a very hazardous material. The danger is that people may breathe in some plutonium dust. It is believed that even a tiny amount of plutonium dust in the lungs could cause cancer. People who work with fast reactors which use plutonium have to be very careful. The material is handled by remote control and kept in concrete or steel containers. If plutonium does have to be handled in a laboratory, it is put into a special 'glove box'. This is a container which is completely leakproof. It incorporates a protective glove into which the scientist can put his arm to handle the material. It is not possible for the plutonium to escape into the outside air.

Power stations have been designed so that workers are not put at risk. If they have to go into parts of the power station where there may be some radiation, they wear protective clothing like the suit in picture [18]. At the end of their shift, they change back into their ordinary clothes. As a worker leaves the

[18]

[19]

changing room, he is checked by a monitor to make sure that he has not been contaminated by radiation, as you can see in picture [19]. Everyone wears a 'film badge' which records their radiation dose.

The whole power station and the atmosphere outside is always being checked for radiation. In a control room at the power station, special instruments are used to check the air. One way of doing this is to draw in samples of air through a filter paper in the machine. Any radioactive particles collect on the paper and can be measured.

How can nuclear waste be disposed of so that there is no risk to people's health?

Radioactive elements gradually decay and lose their radioactivity. This takes many years to happen but, if waste materials can be stored very safely, in time they will no longer be dangerous.

There are three levels of radioactive waste. The most radioactive of all is the uranium which cannot be recycled. This is called high-level waste. It is stored in special tanks enclosed in concrete vaults. The plan is to keep it for at least fifty years so that it cools down and its level of radioactivity declines. This material could be sealed into solid glass blocks and stored deep in the ground or under the ocean bed.

How much waste are we talking about? Imagine that one person uses electricity generated by nuclear power for the whole of his life. The nuclear waste from all the electricity produced for this one person would fit into a small glass block like the one in picture [20]. The waste collected in most nuclear-using countries during the last 30 years would only fill two or three average-sized houses.

The liquids from the cooling ponds and the fuel containers which I told you about in chapter 2 are called medium-level wastes. They are not so radioactive as the uranium waste from the used fuel rods. At the moment, medium-level wastes are stored in sealed units, but studies are being made to see if they could be buried deep underground.

Low-level wastes include plastic and paper

[20]

materials from workshops and laboratories, clothing and protective equipment used by power station workers, and some liquid and gas wastes. Picture [21] shows the sort of thing you would find in a bin of low-level waste. These are put into containers and buried underground or in the deep oceans. Some low-level liquid is discharged into the sea, and low-level gas is released into the atmosphere. This is very strictly controlled by government policies. It should not be any more dangerous than the natural radioactivity which is all around us.

[21]

I have already told you that some low-level wastes are released into the environment. Checks are made outside the power stations to make sure that these are doing no harm. Some low-level liquids are pumped into rivers and the sea, therefore seaweed, water, fish, and shellfish are all checked to see that levels of radiation are not rising. The men in picture [22] are collecting water samples for analysis.

[22]

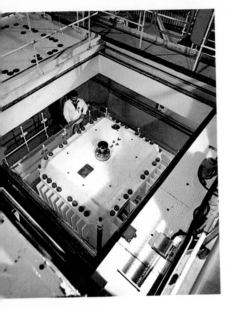

[23]

Samples of foods like milk are analysed in areas near nuclear power stations. All in all, the safety regulations for nuclear power are much stricter than they are for other industries. Hardly any radioactive materials have escaped during the thirty years since nuclear power stations began.

Lots of things in life carry some risk. If you cross the road, you may be run over by a car. You need to cross the road, so you take the risk. Scientists believe that the risks involved in using nuclear power are very small. The miners who get the uranium out of the rock run a slight risk. Uranium is radioactive and the miners might be affected. But the dangers of mining coal are greater. There are poisonous gases underground, tunnels can collapse, coal dust in the lungs can cause disease. Coal mining has been going on for some time—far longer than uranium mining. We have got used to the fact that there are risks involved.

The uranium and waste materials have to be transported around the countryside. The spent fuel has to be taken from the power stations to the reprocessing plant. It is transported by road or rail in 50-tonne flasks, like the one in picture [23]. A test in Britain in 1984 showed that a crash at 160 kph would not damage these flasks. Radioactive material has to be shipped from country to country and no radiation hazards have been caused by doing this.

Nothing we do is absolutely safe. However, concern about radiation causes us to keep a very close eye on nuclear power stations, and the way they are run.

5 · *The future for nuclear power*

You may be wondering why we bother with a material that could be dangerous. Would it not be better just to forget the whole thing and find some other method of generating electricity?

Scientists do not think so. I have already told you about the problem with coal and oil—they will not last for ever. You can see from earlier chapters in this book that uranium is a far more economical fuel. It does not burn away and so it can be recycled until the atoms that will split have all been used up. Picture [24] shows a scene inside one of the reprocessing plants. Fast reactors which use

[24]

plutonium can go on and on reproducing fuel from the same uranium rods. Uranium is too valuable to waste, and it cannot be used in any other way. Several countries think that it makes sense to build nuclear power stations and save their coal and oil for other things.

At the moment there are very few nuclear power stations compared with the number of coal or oil-fired power stations. There are just over 200 nuclear power stations in the world, in thirty-two countries. It is likely that forty countries will be using nuclear power by the end of this century. Dwindling supplies of oil and coal is not the only reason. The population of the world is increasing, and people are using more electricity than ever before. Most of the machines we use these days are run on electricity. In some countries, work that used to be done by hand until quite recently is now done by machines, so the need for electricity will go on increasing.

In picture [25] you can see another nuclear power station being built. The countries which already have nuclear power stations are building more which use the fission process (splitting atoms). Several countries are also carrying out research into nuclear fusion. Experimental devices for heating the gas to the required temperatures are being built in the United States, Russia, Japan, and Britain.

Other uses of nuclear radiation

Because radiation can penetrate solid substances, such as the human body, it can be useful in many ways. Gamma radiation is used in hospitals. The rays kill cancer cells. They

[25]

also kill bacteria, so they are used to sterilize medical equipment like syringes and scalpel blades. Radiation of this sort is very low-level, but is carefully controlled so that it does not harm anyone.

I have already mentioned that radiation is used to see into the human body, in the form of x-rays. Another important use is checking underwater structures like oil rigs, to make sure that they are not corroding or wearing out. Radiation can measure the thickness of materials and examine for cracks and flaws. Aircraft are sometimes checked with radioactive devices which can discover faults deep inside the body or engines.

Nuclear power is a complicated subject. You really need to be a nuclear scientist to understand it fully. But it is part of our modern age, and one which we shall be using for centuries to come. So aren't you glad you have taken the trouble to learn how it works?

Index

advanced gas-cooled reactor
 14–16
Alpha rays 19, 21–2
atoms 3, 7–10, 13, 19
Australia 3, 6, 7, 11–12

Beta rays 19, 22
boron 14, 16
Britain 6, 28, 30

cadmium 14, 16
Canada 3, 6, 7, 12
chain reaction 10, 13
coal 3, 4, 5
coolant 14

economy of use 11
electricity 3, 4, 5
electrons 8, 21
Energy from Sun, Wind, and
 Tide 6

fast reactors 13, 16–18
fission 7, 9, 30

France 6
fuel rods 13–18
fusion 10, 30

Gamma rays 19, 22, 30
generators 4, 5, 6
Germany 8

ions 19

Japan 6, 30

Magnox reactors 14
mining for uranium 3, 11, 28
moderator 13
monitoring for radioactivity 22,
 25

neutrons 8–10, 13, 19, 21
North Africa 7, 12
nuclear bomb 24
nuclear fission 7, 9
nuclear fusion 10
nuclear reactors 13–17
nuclear waste 26–8
nucleus of an atom 8

oil 3, 4, 5

plutonium 13, 16, 24
power stations

coal and oil fired 3, 5
 nuclear 3, 6–10, 12–18, 24,
  30
 number of 30
 pressurized water reactor
  14–16
protons 8–10, 19, 21

radiation 4, 19–23, 24–8
 non-nuclear uses 20, 30–31
radiation therapy 20
radioactivity 18, 19–23, 24–8
reactors 13–17
recycling 17–18
reprocessing plant 18, 29
Russia 6, 30

safety regulations 27–8
splitting of atoms 9–10
stable and unstable atoms 19

thermal reactors 13–16
transportation of nuclear fuel
 and waste 28

uranium 3, 7, 11–18
uranium 235 and 238 atoms
 9–10, 12–17, 24
U.S.A. 6, 7, 12, 14, 30

x-rays 20

Acknowledgements for photographs: Australian Information Services, London 11; British Nuclear Fuels plc, 8, 12, 15, 17, 18 (both), 20, 21, 23, 28, 29; Central Electricity Generating Board, picture on Contents page, and pages 5, 6, 7, 25, 31; United Kingdom Atomic Energy Authority, pictures on Cover and Title page, and pages 3, 9, 13, 16, 24, 26, 27 (both).